PUFFIN BOOKS

THE WITCHES: Plays for Children

Roald Dahl was born in 1916 in Wales of Norwegian parents. He was educated in England before start-ing work for the Shell Oil Company in Africa. He began writing after a 'monumental bash on the head' sustained as an RAF fighter pilot during the Second World War. Roald Dahl is one of the most successful and well known of all children's writers. His books, which are read by children the world over, include *James and the Giant Peach*, *Charlie and the Chocolate Factory*, *The Magic Finger*, *Charlie and the Great Glass Elevator*, *Fantastic Mr Fox*, *Matilda*, *The Twits*, *The BFG* and *The Witches*, winner of the 1983 Whitbread Award. Roald Dahl died in 1990 at the age of seventy-four.

ROALD DAHL'S

The Witches

Plays for Children

✳ ✳ ✳ ✳ ✳ ✳ ✳ ✳

Adapted by David Wood

PUFFIN BOOKS

PUFFIN BOOKS

Published by the Penguin Group
Penguin Books Ltd, 80 Strand, London WC2R 0RL, England
Penguin Putnam Inc., 375 Hudson Street, New York, New York 10014, USA
Penguin Books Australia Ltd, 250 Camberwell Road, Camberwell, Victoria 3124, Australia
Penguin Books Canada Ltd, 10 Alcorn Avenue, Toronto, Ontario, Canada M4V 3B2
Penguin Books India (P) Ltd, 11 Community Centre, Panchsheel Park, New Delhi – 110 017, India
Penguin Books (NZ) Ltd, Cnr Rosedale and Airborne Roads, Albany, Auckland, New Zealand
Penguin Books (South Africa) (Pty) Ltd, 24 Sturdee Avenue, Rosebank 2196, South Africa

Penguin Books Ltd, Registered Offices: 80 Strand, London WC2R 0RL, England

www.penguin.com

First published in Puffin Books 2001

9

Text copyright © Roald Dahl Nominee Ltd and David Wood, 2001
Illustrations copyright © Strawberrie Donnelly, 2001
All rights reserved

The moral right of the authors and illustrator has been asserted

Set in Monotype Bembo
Typeset by Rowland Phototypesetting Ltd, Bury St Edmunds, Suffolk

Made and printed in England by Clays Ltd, St Ives plc

British Library Cataloguing in Publication Data
A CIP catalogue record for this book is available from the British Library

ISBN 0–141–31084–7

Performance Rights:
All rights whatsoever in these plays are strictly reserved, and application for performance, etc.,
should be made before rehearsals commence to: for amateur stage performances, Samuel French
Limited, 52 Fitzroy Street, London W1P 6JR; for all other performance rights to Casarotto Ramsay
& Associates Ltd, National House, 60 Wardour Street, London W1V 4ND.

No performances may be given unless a licence has been obtained. The publications of these plays
does not necessarily indicate their availability for performance.

CONTENTS

Thank you, Justin Savage and James Woods of Clarion Productions for originally commissioning me to adapt the full-length play *The Witches*, and for producing it in London's West End and on tour.

Working with me on that first professional production was a splendid production team, without whom it would have been very difficult to translate *The Witches* to the stage. Their creative input enhanced my original conception and helped solve many tricky staging problems. So heartfelt thanks to Susie Caulcutt (designer), Paul Kieve (illusionist), Sheila Falconer (director of movement), Peter Pontzen (music composer), Mike Furness (sound designer), the late John Thirtle (puppet maker), Simon Courtenay-Taylor (lighting designer) and all the cast; their contribution is reflected in *The Witches: Plays for Children*.

David Wood

FOREWORD

Out of all Roald's books, *The Witches* should be my favourite. Why? Because he dedicated it to me. Occasionally, I wondered what his reasons were. However, the first time I met John Cleese, he said to me that he thought this book was the greatest love story in the world. This stopped me worrying.

Not many of you will know that this book was a tribute to Roald's Norwegian mother who, like the grandmother in *The Witches*, was a very brave and intrepid woman. Her husband died when she was very young, leaving her with two step-children, three of her own children and a baby on the way. She had to bring them all up alone in a country foreign to her (Britain), with a language that she found difficult to speak (English).

Each summer she would pack up their trunks and catch a train to Newcastle to take them all to Norway for their holidays on the island of Töme. In his book *Boy*, Roald describes excursions in a funny little white motor boat, his mother calmly handling the tiller 'with waves so high that as we slid down into a trough the whole world disappeared'. She could not swim and there were no life-jackets. No wonder he created the grandmother in *The Witches* as a woman capable of handling any situation, including that of a boy being turned into a mouse.

Imagine being a mouse and spending the rest of your life in a handbag. Roald used to say that good mothers always kept treats in their bags: wine gums, Polo mints or the odd toffee, among the lipstick and spare handkerchiefs. So I suppose it could be quite a comfortable mobile home.

What a challenge it would be for a parent to have a child turned into a mouse! An enormous amount of imagination would be needed to make life interesting and fun. Roald had quite an affection for mice. From where he sat in the dining-room, he would watch the mice in the heather bed outside his window. He would refer to them as 'the mices'. I think he too might have coped quite well if his children had been transformed into mice.

And why did John Cleese call it a love story? I think you will discover the answer at the very end of this book of plays.

Felicity Dahl

INTRODUCTION

'It's been the best week of my life,' said one of the witches of Sheffield. She had just finished taking part in my professional adaptation of Roald Dahl's classic book. Like many of the fifteen local witches in the production, she had never set foot on a stage before, but suddenly discovered what fun acting could be. We toured the show all over the UK for a year or more and spent two Christmas seasons in London's West End. Hundreds of amateur actresses, ranging in age between fourteen and eighty-four, joined us, fifteen at each theatre, and took the chance to play alongside our professional cast. Not only did they make the Witches' Annual Meeting come thrillingly alive but also they found themselves magically transformed into mice at the end.

It made me realize just how enjoyable being in a play can be – for everybody, not just for those of us who have chosen it as a career. And, in *The Witches*, Dahl, the master story-teller, has given us a highly theatrical tale, ripe for adaptation and performance. It has humour, horror, magic, the triumph of good over evil and, at its heart, a story of warmth and affection between a young boy and his grandmother.

These days few schools, drama clubs or youth groups have the time or resources to mount a full-length play. It seemed like a good idea to create some shorter plays around the most exciting incidents in the story. Some involve just a few people; some could involve a whole class. Some are more complicated to stage than others, but all are meaty enough to provide a rewarding experience for the actors and the audience.

I hope you have fun with them.

David Wood

REAL WITCHES

This play has been written for twenty actors; however, it would be possible to perform with more or fewer. Boy and Grandmother are large acting roles. The other actors perform as a group or chorus, and some of them also play smaller roles. This scene could be an ideal introduction to acting out a story, perhaps encouraging the group to go on to tackle a more complex play.

CHARACTERS
Most of the actors can wear their own clothes or a basic 'uniform' like jeans and T-shirts. Grandmother could wear a long dress and apron. Boy could wear a shirt and short trousers, Mama a dress and Papa a jacket. The Real Witches need to look like 'ordinary women'; special requirements are gloves, handbags, wigs (both bald and hairy) and stockings made to look toeless. False finger-nails could represent claws. 'Blue spit' can be created with dentist's disclosing fluid!

SETTING
An empty space.

PROPS
Grandmother's table and chair. Resting on the table is a large antique-looking book.
Grandmother's thin cigar, matches and ashtray.

3

SOUND EFFECTS

It is suggested that the 'chorus' make all the sounds vocally, for example the accelerating car. Percussion instruments could be used as appropriate.

LIGHTING

Nothing special is required, but it would be effective to be able to brighten 'Grandmother's room' and the 'Real Witches area'. Also, when the 'blue spit' is revealed, general blue lighting could enhance the moment.

REAL WITCHES

Curtain up.

The CAST *assemble in a semicircle. As the action progresses, some of the* ACTORS *will step forward to play their parts, then step back again.* GRANDMOTHER's *table and chair are to one side. Fanfare.*

ALL: The Witches, by Roald Dahl.
[*Fanfare*]

The beginning of the story.
[*Fanfare*]

Real Witches.

ACTOR 1: Christmas holidays.

ACTOR 2: Winter sunshine.

ACTOR 3: Happy.

ACTOR 4: North of Oslo.

ACTOR 5: [*Moving forward, kneeling and miming driving*]
Papa driving.
[GROUP 1 *start humming to suggest a car engine, growing louder as the drama intensifies*]

ACTOR 6: [*Moving forward, kneeling beside 'Papa'*]
Mama beside him.

5

ACTOR 7: [*Moving forward, standing behind 'Mama' and 'Papa'*] Me in the back.

ACTOR 8: Icy road.

GROUP 2: [*Echo*] Icy road.

ACTOR 9: Skidding.

GROUP 2: [*Echo*] Skidding.

ACTOR 10: Sliding.

GROUP 2: [*Echo*] Sliding.

ACTOR 11: Out of control.

GROUP 2: [*Echo*] Out of control.

ACTOR 12: Off the road.

GROUP 2: [*Echo*] Off the road.

ACTOR 13: Tumbling.

GROUP 2: [*Echo*] Tumbling. [*The climax*] Into a rocky ravine.
[*Silence*]
[ALL *lower their heads, to suggest the car crash*]

ACTOR 7 (BOY): [*A horrified cry*] Mama! Papa! No!
[*He comes forward and runs into the arms of* ACTOR 14 (GRANDMOTHER), *who comes to meet him in front of her table and chair.* ACTORS 5 *and* 6 *return to the semicircle*]

GRANDMOTHER: [*Enfolding* BOY *in her arms*] Sob your heart out, darling Boy. Grandmamma's here.

BOY: What are we going to do now?

GRANDMOTHER: You will stay here with me. And I will look after you.

BOY: Aren't I going back to England?

GRANDMOTHER: No. I could never do that. Heaven shall take my soul, but Norway shall keep my bones.
[*They continue hugging.* GRANDMOTHER *turns to the audience*]

As the days passed, time began to heal the hurt.
[*She leads* BOY *to her chair. She sits. He kneels at her feet*]

Each evening I told him stories of summer holidays when I was young. [*To* BOY] We used to row out in a boat and wave to the shrimp boats on their way home. They would stop and give us a handful of shrimps each, still warm from having just been cooked. We peeled them and gobbled them up. The head was the best part.
[BOY *looks interested*]

BOY: The head?

GRANDMOTHER: You squeeze it between your teeth and suck out the inside. [*She demonstrates with relish*]

ALL: [*Echo the sucking sound*]

GRANDMOTHER: It's marvellous.

BOY: [*Enjoying the horror*] Ugggggh! It's horrible!

GRANDMOTHER: [*Lighting a thin black cigar*] Horrible things can be exciting, Boy. Take . . . witches.

BOY: Witches? With silly black hats and black cloaks, riding on broomsticks?

GRANDMOTHER: No. They're for fairy-tales. I'm talking of *real* witches.

BOY: *Real* witches?

ALL: *Real* witches?

GRANDMOTHER: Real witches.

ALL: Real witches.

GRANDMOTHER: Real witches dress in ordinary clothes and look very much like ordinary women. That's why they're so hard to catch.

BOY: But why should we want to catch them?

GRANDMOTHER: Because, my darling Boy, they are evil. They hate children. They get the same pleasure from squelching a child as you get from eating a plateful of strawberries and thick cream.

BOY: Squelching?

[ACTORS 15 *and* 16 *mime* GRANDMOTHER'S *following speech, one playing a witch, the other her victim*]

GRANDMOTHER: She chooses a victim, softly stalks it. Closer and closer, then . . . phwisst! . . . she swoops.

ALL (*except* BOY) *join in with* GRANDMOTHER:
[*Building to a climax*] Sparks fly. Flames leap. Oil boils. Rats howl. Skin shrivels . . .

GRANDMOTHER: And the child disappears.

ALL: Squelched.
[ACTORS 15 *and* 16 *return to the semicircle*]

BOY: Disappears?
[*During the following speech,* ACTOR 17 *moves forward and mimes becoming a chicken. This should complement not swamp* GRANDMOTHER'S *speech!*]

GRANDMOTHER: Not always. Sometimes the child is transformed into something else. Like little Birgit Svenson who lived across the road from us. One day she started growing feathers all over her body. Within a month she had turned into a large white chicken. Her parents kept her for years in a pen in the garden. She even laid eggs.

BOY: What colour eggs?

GRANDMOTHER: Brown ones. Biggest eggs I've ever seen. Her mother made omelettes out of them. Delicious, they were.

[ACTOR 17 *returns to the semicircle*]

BOY: Are you being truthful, Grandmamma? Really and truly truthful? Not pulling my leg.

GRANDMOTHER: My darling Boy, you won't last long in this world if you don't know how to spot a witch when you see one.

BOY: Then tell me. Please!

ALL: Please! PLEASE!

[*Slowly* GRANDMOTHER *takes a large book from the table and opens it to show* BOY *a picture. As she finds the page,* ACTORS 18, 19 *and* 20 (REAL WITCHES) *step forward, looking like ordinary women*]

BOY: [*Looking at the book*] They don't look like witches.

GRANDMOTHER: Of course not. If witches looked like witches we could round them all up and put them in the meat-grinder. But look, there's a clue. They're wearing gloves.

BOY: Mama used to wear gloves.

GRANDMOTHER: Not in the summer, when it's hot. Not in the house. Witches do.

BOY: Why?

GRANDMOTHER: Because they don't have finger-nails.

[*The* REAL WITCHES, *almost in choreographed slow motion, remove a glove*]

They have thin, curvy claws, like a cat.

[*The* REAL WITCHES *gesture threateningly with their claws*]

BOY: Uggggh!

ALL: Uggggh!

GRANDMOTHER: Second clue. They wear wigs. Real witches are always bald.

[*The* REAL WITCHES *remove their wigs, revealing bald heads*]

Not a single hair grows on their heads.

BOY: Horrid.

GRANDMOTHER: Disgusting.

ALL: Disgusting.

[*The* REAL WITCHES *begin to scratch their bald heads*]

GRANDMOTHER: And the wigs give them nasty sores on the head. Wig-rash, it's called. And it doesn't half itch.

BOY: What else, Grandmamma?

GRANDMOTHER: Big nose-holes.

[*The* REAL WITCHES *raise their heads and flare their nostrils*]

BOY: What for?

GRANDMOTHER: To sniff out the stink-waves of children.

BOY: I don't give out stink-waves, do I?

GRANDMOTHER: Not to me, you don't. To me you smell like raspberries and cream. But to a witch you smell – all children smell – like fresh dogs' droppings.

ALL: Fresh dogs' droppings.

BOY: Dogs' droppings? I don't believe it.

GRANDMOTHER: So, if you see a woman holding her nose as she passes you in the street, that woman could easily be a witch. Now, look at their feet.

BOY: Nothing special about them.

GRANDMOTHER: Wrong. They have no toes.
[*The* REAL WITCHES *each take off a shoe, revealing a stockinged stub*]

BOY: Uggggh!

ALL: Uggggh!

GRANDMOTHER: And last but not least, witches have blue spit.

[*The* REAL WITCHES *smile for the first time, revealing a haze of blue teeth. They cackle menacingly*]

ALL: [*Echo the cackle*]
[*The* REAL WITCHES *return to the semicircle*]

GRANDMOTHER: [*Closing the book*] So, my darling Boy, now you know.

ALL: Now you know. Now you know.

[*Curtain down*]

THE TREE-HOUSE WITCH

This play offers three meaty roles, plus a narrated introduction. Some of the dialogue from the previous play has deliberately been included, to cater for three more experienced actors working without a 'chorus'. Performed with concentration and a good sense of tension and atmosphere, this play is really spooky.

CHARACTERS

Narrator

Grandmother: wearing her dress and apron

Boy: wearing his shirt and short trousers

The Tree-House Witch: wearing a wig, an ordinary dress and shoes, carrying a handbag with her snake inside; when she smiles, her teeth should look blue.

SETTING

On one side is Grandmother's chair; her table, with an ashtray on it, is optional. On the other side is the tree-house, the basis of which could be a set of step-ladders; the top could be the platform of the house, foliage or painted canvas could suggest the tree.

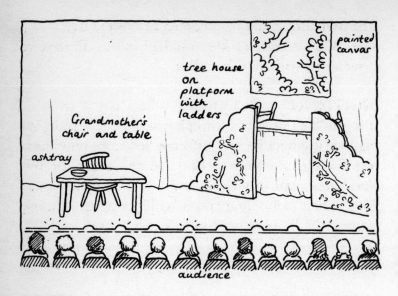

PROPS

Grandmother's cigars, matches and ashtray; a torch.

Boy's plank and hammer.

The Tree-House Witch's snake, which could be one of those segmented toys that looks very realistic when moved.

SOUND EFFECTS

Bird-song could be recorded or created with a percussion instrument.

Time-passing music could be 'tick-tocks' on a wood block.

An optional, but effective, extra could be keyboard music to create tension as the Tree-House Witch pursues Boy.

The owl hoot could be recorded or created live.
The Witch's final cackle could be most effective if
  recorded with an echo effect.

LIGHTING

It is possible to perform this play with no special lighting, but it would be very effective to create two areas,
one for Grandmother's chair and the other for the
tree-house, and to cross-fade from one to the other.
Also, when night-time falls it would help the atmosphere if the lighting were to fade right down low.

THE TREE-HOUSE WITCH

NARRATOR: When Boy's parents die in a car crash in Norway, their will insists he should continue his education in England. So his Norwegian Grandmother comes back too. From her, Boy learns things he would never learn at school. Exciting things, horrible things . . .

[*Curtain up.* GRANDMOTHER *sits on her chair to one side.* BOY *sits at her feet*]

GRANDMOTHER: [*Smoking a long, black cigar*] Take . . . witches.

BOY: Witches? With silly black hats and black cloaks, riding on broomsticks?

GRANDMOTHER: No. They're for fairy-tales. I'm talking of *real* witches.

BOY: *Real* witches?

GRANDMOTHER: Real witches look very much like ordinary women. That's why they're so hard to catch.

BOY: But why should we want to catch them?

GRANDMOTHER: Because, my darling Boy, they are evil. They hate children. They get the same pleasure from squelching a child as you get from eating a plateful of strawberries and thick cream.

BOY: Squelching?

GRANDMOTHER: [*Forcefully stubbing out her cigar*] Squelching.

BOY: Are you being truthful, Grandmamma? Really and truly truthful? Not pulling my leg.

GRANDMOTHER: My darling Boy, you won't last long in this world if you don't know how to spot a witch when you see one.

BOY: Then tell me, please!

GRANDMOTHER: She always wears gloves.

BOY: Why?

GRANDMOTHER: Because she doesn't have finger-nails. She has thin, curvy claws, like a cat.

BOY: Uggggh!

GRANDMOTHER: She wears a wig. A real witch is always bald. Not a single hair grows on her head.

BOY: Horrid.

GRANDMOTHER: Disgusting.

BOY: What else, Grandmamma?

GRANDMOTHER: She has big nose-holes.

BOY: What for?

GRANDMOTHER: To sniff out the stink-waves of children.

BOY: I don't give out stink-waves, do I?

GRANDMOTHER: Not to me, you don't. To me you smell like raspberries and cream. But to a witch you smell – all children smell – like fresh dogs' droppings.

BOY: Dogs' droppings? I don't believe it.

GRANDMOTHER: And a real witch has . . . blue spit.

BOY: Uggggh! Grandmamma . . .

GRANDMOTHER: Yes? [*She lights another thin cigar*]

BOY: Are there any witches in England?

GRANDMOTHER: Of course. Every country has its own Secret Society of Witches.

BOY: I'm sure I won't meet one.

GRANDMOTHER: I sincerely hope you won't. English witches are probably the most vicious in the whole world.

BOY: What do they do?

GRANDMOTHER: Their favourite ruse is to mix up a powder that turns a child into a creature all grown-ups hate.

BOY: Such as?

GRANDMOTHER: A slug. Then the grown-ups step on the slug and squish it without knowing it's a child, *their* child maybe.

BOY: That's awful.

GRANDMOTHER: That's English witches for you.

BOY: These . . . Societies of Witches. Do they have meetings? Like our Chess Society at school?

GRANDMOTHER: They have an annual meeting, attended by the Grand High Witch of all the world.

BOY: The Grand High Witch!
[GRANDMOTHER *gets up and exits, leaving* BOY *thoughtful. Then he stands and talks to the audience*]

Soon life was back to sort of normal. We lived in our old house and I went back to school. One Saturday afternoon, when my friend Timmy was in bed with flu, I decided to do some work on the tree-house we were building at the bottom of the garden . . .
[*A bird-song sound effect*]
[BOY *crosses to the tree-house, climbs up and starts nailing a plank*]
[*After a pause, the* TREE-HOUSE WITCH *enters. She sniffs, her nostrils flared. She traces the scent, looking up to* BOY*, who works on, unaware. The bird-song stops*]

24

[*Tension mounts as the* TREE-HOUSE WITCH *slowly starts to climb the steps to the tree-house*]

[BOY *is still hammering the nail. Just as it seems the* TREE-HOUSE WITCH *might reach him, he accidentally drops the hammer with a clatter. The* TREE-HOUSE WITCH *retreats a little*]

[BOY *descends to fetch his hammer. He picks it up, turns, and suddenly sees the* TREE-HOUSE WITCH. *He stops*]

WITCH: [*Waving a gloved hand*] Hello, boy.
[*She smiles a blue smile*]

Don't be shy. I have a present for you.
[BOY, *nervous, starts to climb the steps*]

Come down out of that tree, boy, and I shall give you the most exciting present you've ever had.
[*Still looking up at* BOY, *she produces, perhaps from her handbag, a thin green snake. It coils itself round her forearm*]

If you come down here, I shall give him to you.
[BOY, *mesmerized by the snake, descends and approaches*]

It's tame. Come, stroke him.
[BOY *goes to stroke the snake. Suddenly the* TREE-HOUSE WITCH *grabs* BOY *by the arm. A struggle ensues. Then* BOY *stamps on the* TREE-HOUSE WITCH'*s foot. She screams with frustration as* BOY *climbs back up to the tree-house to hide*]

[THE TREE-HOUSE WITCH *calms herself, then leaves, cackling horribly*]
[*The lights fade. Time-passing music. An owl hoots*]

GRANDMOTHER: [*Off*] Boy!
[GRANDMOTHER *enters with a torch*]

Boy!

BOY: [*From the tree-house*] Grandmamma. Up here.

GRANDMOTHER: Come down at once. It's past your supper-time.

BOY: Has that woman gone?

GRANDMOTHER: What woman?

BOY: The woman in the black gloves.
[GRANDMOTHER *is stunned*]

GRANDMOTHER: Gloves?

BOY: [*Urgently*] Has she gone?
[GRANDMOTHER *searches with her torch around the tree-house*]

GRANDMOTHER: Yes, she's gone. I'm here, my darling.
[BOY *descends gingerly. Then, trembling, he falls into* GRANDMOTHER'*s arms*]

There, there. I'll look after you.

BOY: [*With an effort*] I've seen a witch.

[*A cackle echoes through the night as the curtain falls*]

THE GRAND HIGH WITCH

A Narrator introduces this play, which has five main roles. Several witches, one of whom has lines to say, enter the Hotel Magnificent as the scene progresses. If more parts are required, two or three witches at a time could enter, rather than just the one mentioned. The broad humour of the first part changes as soon as the Grand High Witch enters, when a feeling of mesmerizing menace takes over.

CHARACTERS
Narrator

Boy: wearing his shirt and short trousers

Hotel Doorman: ideally wearing peaked cap and frock-coat with brass buttons

Bruno Jenkins: dressed in T-shirt and shorts

Mr Jenkins: with a black moustache, wearing a suit and flashy tie

Mrs Jenkins: looking rather tastelessly overdressed

The Grand High Witch: dressed very smartly in a black suit and hat with a veil

Witches: all looking ordinary but obviously wearing wigs.

SETTING

All that is necessary is a doorway. The door itself could be imagined. If possible, the doorway is set on a rostrum, giving a step up to the entrance. Above the door could be a sign saying 'Hotel Magnificent'. The front walls either side of the door can be imagined; as people go through the door, they can simply exit upstage of it.

PROPS

Bruno's cream bun in a paper bag.

Bruno's magnifying-glass.

Boy's box containing two white mice. The mice can be imagined, but it would be fun if a mouse-head could pop up from the box when its lid is removed.

30

A doughnut in a paper bag.

The Grand High Witch's handbag, in which is a bar
of chocolate.

SOUND EFFECTS
Recorded or created seagull cries can be heard
sparingly throughout the play, until the arrival of
the Grand High Witch.
Recorded sea sounds are optional.

LIGHTING
No special lighting is required. However, ideally the
area upstage of the hotel entrance should be dimly
lit, to contrast with the brightness downstage. Also, it
would be effective to dim the lighting somewhat as
the Grand High Witch enters.

THE GRAND HIGH WITCH

NARRATOR: When Boy's parents die in a car crash, his Norwegian Grandmother comes to look after him. She tells him about witches, not the flying-on-broomsticks fairy-tale variety, rather *real* witches, who hate children and enjoy using their magic skills to get rid of them. They disguise themselves as ordinary women to avoid capture, and once a year they attend a special meeting, attended by the Grand High Witch of all the World. Boy is upset when Grandmother becomes ill. The doctor says that sea air will do her good . . .

[*Curtain up, revealing* BOY *outside the hotel entrance; seagull cries*]

BOY: And that's how we came to stay in Bournemouth. At the Hotel Magnificent.

[BOY *indicates the hotel and exits*]

[*The* HOTEL DOORMAN *comes out of the doorway. He sniffs the air and struts about pompously*]

[BRUNO JENKINS *enters and stands near the* DOORMAN, *cheekily imitating his stance and making rude faces. He laughs at the* DOORMAN, *who is trying not to react to the rudeness.* BRUNO *then sits on the step, removes a cream bun from a paper bag, and provocatively starts eating it*]

[*A* LADY (WITCH) *enters and tries to go into the*

hotel. BRUNO *is in her way. She tries to get round him, but he slides himself along the step to block her path]*

LADY: Excuse me.

BRUNO: [*Rudely*] Why? What've you done?

LADY: Pardon me?

BRUNO: Granted.
[*He laughs rudely*]

LADY: Move, please.

BRUNO: Shan't. So there.
[*The* DOORMAN *approaches*]

DOORMAN: Shift yourself, sunshine.
[*He pushes* BRUNO, *whose face hits the cream bun*]

BRUNO: [*Spluttering*] Hey!

DOORMAN: Good-day, madam.

LADY: Thank you.
[*The door is held open by the* DOORMAN. *The* LADY *enters the hotel*]

BRUNO: [*To the* DOORMAN] I'll set my dad on you.

DOORMAN: [*Impassively*] I can't wait.
[*Another* LADY (WITCH) *arrives*]

Good-day, madam. Straight through for the meeting.

[*He opens the door. Before the* LADY *can go in,* MR JENKINS *emerges from inside and pushes rudely through*]

MR JENKINS: [*Loudly*] Bruno.

BRUNO: Yes, Dad.
[*The* LADY *manages to go in*]

DOORMAN: [*Long suffering*] Can I help you, Mr Jenkins?

MR JENKINS: No, you can't. You lot only help if there's a tip at the end of it. Beat it, Buttons.

BRUNO: Yes, beat it, Buttons! [*He laughs*]

DOORMAN: As you please, sir.
[*He goes inside*]

MR JENKINS: Shut up, Bruno. Where's your ma?

BRUNO: Gone to buy me a doughnut.

MR JENKINS: You'll turn into a doughnut, you fat slob.

BRUNO: So?

MR JENKINS: Tell your ma I'm in the bar.
[*He turns to go*]

BRUNO: Getting drunk time, is it, Pa?

MR JENKINS: [*Stopping by the door*] What?

BRUNO: I said, 'Nearly lunch-time, is it, Pa?'

MR JENKINS: Watch it.
[*Another* LADY (WITCH) *approaches. The* DOOR-
MAN *opens the door from the inside, knocking into* MR
JENKINS]

[*To the* DOORMAN] Watch it.

DOORMAN: [*Sweetly*] So sorry, Mr Jenkins.
[MR JENKINS *rudely pushes inside ahead of the lady*]

MR JENKINS: [*To the* LADY] Watch it.

DOORMAN: Good-day, madam. Straight through.
[BRUNO *takes out a magnifying-glass and focuses it on
the step.* BOY *enters, carrying a box*]

BOY: Hello, Bruno.

BRUNO: What you got in there? Something to eat?
Give us some.

BOY: I've been to the pet shop. Grandmamma gave
me some money.

BRUNO: What've you got?

BOY: White mice. I'm going to call them William and
Mary.

BRUNO: Boring. Guess what pets I got.

BOY: What?

BRUNO: Chinchillas and mink.

BOY: Oh?

BRUNO: Gonna make me ma a fur coat, see.

BOY: Oh.
    [*Another* LADY (WITCH) *arrives, steps over* BRUNO *and enters the hotel*]

BRUNO: [*Concentrating on his magnifying-glass now*] Bet my dad earns more than yours.

BOY: Probably.

BRUNO: How many cars has he got, your dad?

BOY: None.

BRUNO: Mine's got three.

BOY: What are you doing with that magnifying-glass?

BRUNO: Roasting ants.

BOY: That's horrible. Stop it.
    [*He tries to grab the magnifying-glass*]

BRUNO: Here. Get away. Shove off.
    [*A scuffle breaks out*]
    [MRS JENKINS *enters, carrying a paper bag*]

MRS JENKINS: Bruno!
    [*She tries to pull the boys apart*]

[*To* BOY] You great bully. [*She slaps hard an arm which she thinks belongs to* BOY, *but which in fact belongs to* BRUNO] Lay off my little Bruno, do you hear?

BRUNO: [*Wailing*] Ow! Mum . . .

MRS JENKINS: [*Going to* BRUNO *and brushing him down*] Look at you, your shorts are all grubby.

BRUNO: He tried to nick my magnifying-glass.

MRS JENKINS: [*To* BOY] You keep away from my little Bruno, d'you hear? [*To* BRUNO] There's your doughnut, treasure.

BRUNO: [*Taking it greedily*] Ask him what's in that box, Ma.

MRS JENKINS: Why? [*To* BOY] Have you nicked that 'n' all?

BOY: No. It's William and Mary.

MRS JENKINS: What d'you mean, William and Mary? Give us a look.
[*She lifts the lid. A mouse's head pops up, or* MRS JENKINS *simply looks inside*]

Ahhhhh! Mice! Aaaaaaaaah!
[*She runs into the hotel, screaming*]

BRUNO: [*Roaring with laughter, calling after her*] Pa's in the bar, Ma. [*But she has gone*] Silly old witch.

BOY: [*alert*] What did you say?

BRUNO: Nothing.

BOY: I'd better go and see Grandmamma.

[*The* DOORMAN *opens the door for him. He enters the hotel*]

[*Another* LADY (WITCH) *enters. She is welcomed by the* DOORMAN *and enters the hotel*]

[BRUNO *sits on the steps and starts eating the doughnut and scooping out jam with his finger*]

[*The* DOORMAN *descends the steps, pretending not to notice* BRUNO. *He takes a deep breath or two of fresh air*]

[*Another* LADY (*The* GRAND HIGH WITCH) *enters. Seagull cries stop. The* DOORMAN *turns and sees her. He reacts as if mesmerized by her*]

DOORMAN: Good–day, madam.

GRAND HIGH WITCH: [*Charming*] Good–day. Is this the correct hotel for the Annual General Meeting of the Royal Society for the Prevention of Cruelty to Children?

DOORMAN: It is indeed, madam. Welcome.
[*He holds the door open for her*]
[*The* GRAND HIGH WITCH *starts to ascend the steps, but suddenly stops. She starts sniffing, as genteelly as possible, and turns to see the source of the stink-waves, which is* BRUNO. *She approaches him*]

GRAND HIGH WITCH: Vell, hello, little man.

BRUNO: Eh?

GRAND HIGH WITCH: You are liking your doughnut, yes?

[BRUNO *nods*]

But vot happens ven it is finished? Vould you like some chocolate?
[*She hands him a bar of chocolate*]

BRUNO: [*Enthusiastically*] Yeah.
[*He breaks off a piece and eats it*]

GRAND HIGH WITCH: Good?

BRUNO: Great.

GRAND HIGH WITCH: Vould you like some more?

BRUNO: Yeah.

GRAND HIGH WITCH: I vill give you six more chocolate bars like that if you vill meet me in the ballroom of this hotel at tventy-five past three.

BRUNO: Six bars! I'll be there.
[*The* GRAND HIGH WITCH *enters the hotel, the door held open by the* DOORMAN]

You bet I'll be there!

[*He greedily stuffs more chocolate into his mouth as the curtain falls*]

THE WITCHES' ANNUAL
MEETING

This play dramatizes perhaps the most memorable scene in the book, the scene in which Bruno Jenkins and Boy are transformed into mice by the Grand High Witch. It involves several good roles, including a large number of witches with no individual speeches, but plenty of chorus speech and action to enjoy. Planning is required to make the illusions as mystifying as possible, but the staging is not too complicated and is well worthwhile. This play is ideal for one whole class to perform.

CHARACTERS
Narrator

Boy: wearing his shirt and short trousers

Head Waiter: wearing smart waistcoat and trousers

Witches (fifteen is an ideal number, though more would be possible): all look like 'ordinary women' but must wear gloves and wigs concealing bald heads; they carry handbags

Witch 1: dressed slightly smarter than the others

Witch 2: one of the crowd

The Grand High Witch: dressed very smartly in a black suit. She wears a wig and also a face-mask, making her look normal, yet glamorous; when she removes the mask it reveals her hideous, wizened, rotting face (the made-up face of the actress)

Bruno Jenkins: dressed in T-shirt and shorts.

SETTING
The hotel ballroom, with chairs in rows ready for the meeting. To achieve the various illusions required, it is suggested that a platform or rostrum be set upstage, with curtains making an exit each side. Steps up to the rostrum onstage as well as offstage may be helpful. Two small tables with table-cloths are downstage right and left. Optional curtains hang beside them.

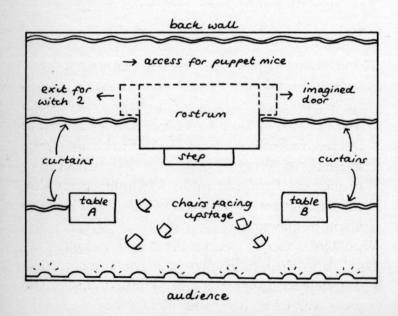

PROPS

A box with holes in the lid (for Boy's white mice).

A large key.

A cushion.

Partly burned remnants of Witch 2's clothes.

A potion bottle.

Board or scroll on which is written the list of ingredients.

A gong and beater.

Two puppet mice (described in Special Effects below).

Two mice (Boy and Bruno) set behind the tables.

SOUND EFFECTS

Throughout this play there are moments when eerie keyboard music could be used to enhance tension and atmosphere. But this is not essential. Percussion sounds could be used for certain moments, such as the removal of the Grand High Witch's mask, the frazzling of Witch 2 and the transformation of Bruno and Boy into mice. Rhythmic percussion accompaniment to the Grand High Witch's chants might be effective.

Woodblocks can be used for the door-knocking.

Loud alarm–clock ringing could be live or recorded. A distorted alarm-bell and clock-chime sound would work well when Boy turns into a mouse.

LIGHTING

No special lighting is essential, but certain effects would be helpful:

- General lighting could brighten when the Witches enter;
- A special red light on Witch 2 as she is frazzled;
- Pulsating light during the transformation of Bruno and Boy into mice.

SPECIAL EFFECTS/MAGICAL ILLUSIONS

THE FRAZZLING OF WITCH 2. She should stand at the back of the platform. A smoke machine (easy to hire from theatrical lighting suppliers) should blow smoke from behind the curtain. The smoke (hopefully lit red) should hide Witch 2, giving her cover to exit behind the curtain. When the smoke clears, she seems to have disappeared.

It would be excellent, when the Grand High Witch gestures towards Witch 2, if sparks could appear to fly from her fingers! 'Hand-flasher' devices are available from magic shops, but they can be dangerous and should be used only under adult supervision.

THE MICE ON THE PLATFORM. William and Mary should be puppet mice (or toy mice mounted on vertical or horizontal rods). They should appear at the back of the platform, operated from behind (if the platform is high enough) or from the sides.

THE TRANSFORMATION OF BRUNO. The Witches summon Bruno to table B. He appears to shrink by ducking down and getting off at the back of the table, under cover of the Witches. He escapes, unseen by the audience, behind the curtain. The Witches step back, revealing a mouse which one of them has picked up from behind the table and set on the table. It may be a good idea to weight the mouse to stop it falling over. And for added sophistication, the mouse could be attached to a wire leading to the back of the table top, enabling a Witch to make the mouse tremble.

If a curtain near the table is impractical, Bruno can hide under the table, which would need to be covered by a table-cloth reaching to the floor.

THE TRANSFORMATION OF BOY. This can be effected in the same way as Bruno's transformation. However, to be more deceptive, the two methods should be different. If Bruno escapes round the curtain, then Boy could hide under the table. Indeed it might be highly effective for the Witches to set the table centre stage, *then* lift Boy on to it. The audience would see that escape offstage either side would be impossible.

THE WITCHES' ANNUAL MEETING

NARRATOR: After Boy's parents are killed in a car crash he goes to live with his Grandmother. She tells him about witches. Real witches who look like ordinary women, but are bald and wear wigs, and who wear gloves to cover their claws. They hate children. To witches, children smell of fresh dogs' droppings. Each year the English Witches hold a meeting attended by the Grand High Witch of all the World. Grandmother suddenly falls ill, very ill. To help her get better, Boy takes her on holiday to Bournemouth, to the Hotel Magnificent.

[*Curtain up*]

One afternoon, Boy explores and finds a colossal room called the Ballroom . . .

[BOY *enters, carrying a box with holes in the lid. He passes through the rows of chairs, then sits on one*]

. . . the perfect place to play with his pet white mice, William and Mary.

[BOY *opens the box and starts to play with the mice*]

[*Suddenly the* HEAD WAITER *enters. The lights could brighten.* BOY *reacts alarmed*]

HEAD WAITER: This way, ladies.

[BOY *hides behind table A as a troupe of ladies* (WITCHES) *enter*]

WITCHES: [*Noisily ad-libbing greetings*]
Oh hello, Beatrice. What an adorable dress! . . .
Agatha, how lovely to see you . . .
Have you had a good journey?
Come and sit next to me, Millie dear . . .
I haven't seen you since the last meeting . . .
[*Etc., etc.*]

[*They arrange themselves, seated facing the platform. As they talk, some scratch their necks with gloved hands*]

[*Eventually the* HEAD WAITER *calls for attention*]

HEAD WAITER: Ladies of the Royal Society for the Prevention of Cruelty to Children, pray welcome your President.
[*Enthusiastic applause. The* GRAND HIGH WITCH *enters in style. She mounts the platform. The* HEAD WAITER *exits*]
[WITCH 1, *bowing to the* GRAND HIGH WITCH, *briefly exits, then returns holding up the door key, to show she has locked the door*]
[*Silence. Slowly the* GRAND HIGH WITCH *removes her wig and then her mask, revealing a wizened, horrible rotting face.* WITCH 1 *receives the wig and the mask on a cushion, then returns to her seat. The other* WITCHES *watch in awe*]

GRAND HIGH WITCH: You may rrree-moof your vigs, and get some fresh air into your spotty scalps.
[*With sighs of relief, the* WITCHES *reveal their bald*

*heads, placing their wigs in handbags or on the floor.
Some scratch their heads*]

Vitches of Inkland. Miserrrable vitches. Useless lazy
vitches. You are a heap of idle good-for-nothing
vurms!

[*A murmur of concern among the* WITCHES]

As I am eating my lunch, I am looking out of the
vindow at the beach. And vot am I seeing? I am
seeing a rrreevolting sight, which is putting me off
my food. Hundreds of rrrotten rrreepulsive children. Playing on the sand. Vye haf you not got rrrid
of them? Vye?

[*No response*]

You vill do better.

WITCH I: [*Standing and encouraging the others*] We will,
your Grandness.

WITCHES: We will do better.

GRAND HIGH WITCH: My orders are that every single
child in Inkland shall be rrrubbed out, sqvashed,
sqvirted, sqvittered and frittered before I come here
again in vun year's time.

[*The* WITCHES *gasp*]

WITCH 2: *All* of them? We can't possibly wipe out *all*
of them.

GRAND HIGH WITCH: Who said that? Who dares to
argue vith me? [*She looks around. The* WITCHES

51

cower. She points dramatically at WITCH 2] It vos you, vos it not?
[WITCH 2 *stands, gasping in fright*]

WITCH 2: I didn't mean it, your Grandness.

GRAND HIGH WITCH: Come here.
[*She beckons.* WITCH 2, *mesmerized, starts to ascend the platform*]

WITCH 2: I didn't mean to argue, your Grandness. I was just talking to myself. I swear it.

GRAND HIGH WITCH:
A vitch who dares to say I'm wrrrong
Vill not be vith us very long!

WITCH 2: Forgive me, your Grandness.
[*She arrives upstage, near the entrance*]

GRAND HIGH WITCH:
A stupid vitch who answers back
Must burn until her bones are black!

WITCH 2: No! No! Spare me!
[*Staring at* WITCH 2, *the* GRAND HIGH WITCH *gestures. Sparks fly. Smoke rises. Red light hits* WITCH 2 *as she writhes*]

Aaaaaaaaaaah!
[WITCH 2 *disappears*]
[*The* WITCHES *utter an awestruck sigh.* BOY, *visible to the audience but not to the* WITCHES, *reacts too*]

GRAND HIGH WITCH: I hope nobody else is going to make me cross today.

[WITCH 1 *tentatively goes upstage and finds the smouldering remnants of* WITCH 2*'s clothes. She holds them up. The* WITCHES *sigh*]

Frrrizzled like a frrritter. Cooked like a carrot. You vill never see her again. Now vee can get down to business.

[*The following sequence should be rhythmic and grow in intensity*]

GRAND HIGH WITCH: Down vith children! Do them in!

WITCHES: Boil their bones and fry their skin!

GRAND HIGH WITCH: Bish them, sqvish them, bash them, mash them!

WITCHES: Break them, shake them, slash them, smash them!

GRAND HIGH WITCH: I am having a plan. A giganticus plan!

WITCHES: She is having a plan. A giganticus plan!

GRAND HIGH WITCH: You vill buy sveetshops.

WITCHES: We will buy sweetshops.

GRAND HIGH WITCH: You vill fill them high vith luscious sveets and tasty chocs!

WITCHES: Luscious sweets and tasty chocs!

GRAND HIGH WITCH: You vill have a Great Gala Opening vith free sveets and chocs for every child!

WITCHES: Free sweets and chocs for every child!
[WITCH I *stands, carried away with enthusiasm*]

WITCH I: I will *poison* the sweets and *poison* the chocs and wipe out the children like weasels.
[*Silence*]

GRAND HIGH WITCH: You vill do no such thing. You brainless bogvumper! Poison them and you vill be caught in five minutes flat. No. Vee vitches are vurrrking only vith magic!

WITCHES: [*Building*] Magic! Magic! Magic!

GRAND HIGH WITCH: You vill be filling every choc and every sveet vith my latest and grrreatest magic formula.
[*A sigh of admiration as she produces a potion bottle*]

Formula Eighty-Six Delayed Action Mouse-Maker!
[*Excited cheers and applause*]

Take down the recipe.
[WITCH I *reveals a board or scroll with the ingredients written on it*]

You vill notice some unusual ingredients: a grrruntle's egg; the claw of a crrrab-crrruncher; the beak of a blabbersnitch; the snout of a grrrobblesqvirt and the tongue of a catsprrringer. Mix them vith forty-five mouse's tails fried in hair-oil till they are crrrisp.

WITCH 1: What do we do with the mice who have had their tails chopped off, your Grandness?

GRAND HIGH WITCH: You simmer them in frog-juice for vun hour. Then you add two secret ingredients. The wrrrong end of a telescope boiled soft . . .

WITCH 1: What's that for, O Brainy One?

GRAND HIGH WITCH: To make a child very small you look at him through the wrrrong end of a tele-scope, do you not?

WITCH 1: [*To the others*] She's a wonder. Who else would have thought of that?

GRAND HIGH WITCH: And finally, to cause the delayed action, rrroast in the oven vun alarm clock set to go off at nine o'clock in the morning.

WITCH 1: A stroke of genius! [*She discards the ingredients list*]

GRAND HIGH WITCH: Inject vun droplet of the formula in each sveet or choc, open your shop, and as the children pour in on their vay home from school . . .
  [*She chants the following rhyme*]

Crrram them full of sticky eats,
Send them home still guzzling sveets,
And in the morning little fools
Go marching off to separate schools.
    [WITCH 1 *bangs a gong nine times*]

A girl feels sick and goes all pale.
She yells, 'Hey, look! I've grrrown a tail!'
A boy who's standing next to her
Screams, 'Help! I think I'm grrrowing fur!'
Another shouts, 'Vee look like frrreaks!
There's viskers growing on our cheeks!'
A boy who vos extremely tall
Cries out, 'Vot's wrong? I'm grrrowing small!'
Four tiny legs begin to sprrrout
From everybody rrround about.
And all at vunce, all in a trrrice,
There are no children! Only mice!
The teachers cry, 'Vot's going on?
Oh, vhere haf all the children gone?'
Then suddenly the mice they spot,
Fetch mousetrrraps strrrong and kill the lot!
They sveep the dead mice all away
And all us vitches shout

ALL: [*Standing*] Hooray!
    [*They rise to a big finish*]

Down vith children! Do them in!
Boil their bones and fry their skin!
Bish them, sqvish them, bash them, mash them!

Brrreak them, shake them, slash them, smash them!
[*The* WITCHES *cheer wildly. They sit again as
the* GRAND HIGH WITCH *acknowledges their
appreciation*]
[*Suddenly* WITCH 1 *leaps up and points to the back of
the platform*]

WITCH 1: Look! Look! Mice!
[*Two white mice are progressing from one side to the
other. They stop nervously, looking about*]

BOY: [*Seeing them from behind the table*] Oh no! William
and Mary!

WITCH 1: Our leader has done it to show us! The
Brainy One has turned two children into mice!
[*The* GRAND HIGH WITCH *has seen the mice. The
other* WITCHES *start to applaud*]

GRAND HIGH WITCH: Qviet!
[*She approaches the mice, who stop moving*]

These mice are nothing to do with me. These mice
are *pet* mice, qvite obviously belonging to some
rrreepellent little child in this hotel.
[*She chases the mice, stamping her feet*]
[*The mice scurry away and disappear*]

WITCH 1: [*Menacingly*] A child! A filthy child. We'll
sniff him out.
[*The* WITCHES *start sniffing and some move
ominously towards the table.* BOY *stiffens*]

[*Then, in the nick of time, there is a knock on the door. The* WITCHES *react, turning away from the table*]

BRUNO: [*Outside the door*] Hey! Let me in!
[*More knocks*]

GRAND HIGH WITCH: Qvick, vitches. Vigs on!
[*The* WITCHES *hurry to make themselves respectable*]

BRUNO: [*Outside the door*] Hurry up! Twenty-five past three you said.

GRAND HIGH WITCH: Vitches. Vatch this demonstrrration. Earlier today I am giving a chocolate bar vith formula added to a smelly boy.

BRUNO: [*Outside the door*] Where's them chocolate bars you promised? I'm here to collect! Dish 'em out!

GRAND HIGH WITCH: Not only smelly but grrreedy. The formula is timed for half past three.
[*She puts on her wig, handed to her by* WITCH 1, *but not her face-mask*]

Let him in.
[WITCH 1 *takes the key and exits upstage to unlock the door*]
[BRUNO *enters and approaches.* WITCH 1 *follows him in*]
[*The* GRAND HIGH WITCH, *keeping her back towards him, comes downstage, off the platform*]

[*Soft and gentle*] Darling little man. I haf your

chocolate all rrready for you. Do come and say hello to all these lovely ladies.

[BRUNO *descends the platform, eyed eagerly by the* WITCHES]

BRUNO: OK, where's my chocolate? Six bars you said.

GRAND HIGH WITCH: [*Checking her watch*] Thirty seconds to go.

BRUNO: What?

[*He receives no reply. He approaches the* GRAND HIGH WITCH]

What the heck's going on?

GRAND HIGH WITCH: Twenty seconds!

BRUNO: [*Getting suspicious*] Gimme the chocolate and let me out of here.

GRAND HIGH WITCH: Fifteen seconds!

BRUNO: [*Looking at the* WITCHES] Will one of you crazy punks kindly tell me what all this is about?

GRAND HIGH WITCH: Ten seconds!

[*She turns her face to* BRUNO, *who reacts with a terrified scream*]

WITCHES: [*Surrounding* BRUNO *menacingly, but also in delighted anticipation*] Nine ... eight ... seven ... six ... five ... four ... three ... two ... one ... zero!

GRAND HIGH WITCH: Vee haf ignition.

[*An alarm clock rings loudly as* BRUNO *is forced on to table B, surrounded by the excited* WITCHES. *He stiffens as the* WITCHES *focus their eyes on him*]

GRAND HIGH WITCH:
This smelly brrrat, this filthy scum
This horrid little louse
Vill very soon become
A lovely little MOUSE!

[*A flash. An eerie sound effect.* BRUNO'*s head darts about like a mouse; his hands, like paws, brush imaginary whiskers. Then he appears to shrink behind the watching* WITCHES]

[*He disappears from view. The* WITCHES *back away from the table.* BRUNO *has gone. In his place on the table-top is a mouse*]

WITCHES: [*Applauding*] Bravo! She's done it! It works! It's fantastic! [*Etc., etc.*]

[*The* GRAND HIGH WITCH *shoos the mouse, swiping it aside with the back of her hand. It appears to make a hurried exit through the* WITCHES, *who react*]

GRAND HIGH WITCH: Vitches, I vill meet you all for dinner at eight. Before dinner, any ancient vuns who can no longer climb high trrrees in search of grrruntles' eggs for the formula may come to my rrrroom. I have prrreepared for you [*She shows the potion bottle*] a bottle each, containing a limited qvantity. Five hundred doses.

WITCHES: [*Led by* WITCH I] Thank you, thank you, your Grandness. How thoughtful.

HIGH WITCH: Room Four-Five-Four. Any qvestions?

WITCH I: One, O Brainy One. What happens if one of the chocolates we are giving away in our shops gets eaten by a grown-up?

GRAND HIGH WITCH: That's just too bad for the grown-up. This meeting is over.
[*The* WITCHES *start to go*]
[*Behind table A* BOY *relaxes, relieved. He stretches and rubs his aching knees*]
[*Suddenly* . . .]

WITCH I: [*Shouting*] Wait! Hold everything.
[*She flares her nostrils, sniffing eagerly. Her face turns towards table A. The* WITCHES *freeze and listen*]
[WITCH I *follows the scent*]

Dogs' droppings. I've got a whiff of fresh dogs' droppings.

GRAND HIGH WITCH: Vot rubbish is this? There are no children in this rrroom!

WITCH I: It's getting stronger. Can't the rest of you smell it? Dogs' droppings.
[ALL *the* WITCHES *are sniffing now*]

WITCHES: Dogs' droppings! Yes! Yes! Dogs' droppings! Dogs' droppings! Poo! Poo-oo-oo-oo-oo!

[*They head towards table A.* BOY *is terrified*]

[WITCH 1 *looks behind the table*]

WITCH 1: [*With a shriek*] Boy! Boy! Boy! Boy!
[*Pandemonium as a chase ensues.* BOY *runs through the* WITCHES, *desperate to escape. He runs anywhere and everywhere. The* WITCHES *chase him. He yells*]

GRAND HIGH WITCH: [*From the platform*] Grrrab it! Stop it yelling! Catch it, you idiots!
[BOY *is surrounded. Helpless, he submits. He is lifted up on to the table*]

Spying little vurm! You stinking little carbuncle. You haf observed the most secret things. Now you must take your medicine!

BOY: Help! Help! Grandmamma!

GRAND HIGH WITCH: Open his mouth!
[*The* WITCHES *do so. Dramatically the* GRAND HIGH WITCH *opens the potion bottle and raises it aloft*]

Five hundred doses! So strrrong vee see INSTANTANEOUS ACTION!
[*She pours the potion into* BOY'*s mouth.* BOY *starts jerking his head. The* WITCHES *surround him*]
[*Strange distorted alarm bells ring. Perhaps the lights pulsate*]
[*Then, as the effects stop, the* WITCHES *step aside*]

[*On the table there is no sign of* BOY. *Just a trembling mouse. The* WITCHES *point and cackle, louder and louder*]

[*Curtain down*]

THE BOY-MOUSE

This play is interesting because it uses two different scales. Boy and Bruno are mice: in two scenes they are played by actors, in one scene they are played by puppets. The major roles are Boy, Bruno and Grand-mother, but there are some enjoyable cameo roles too, including the Grand High Witch, who is never seen, only heard! The staging is a little more complex than in the other plays, but it could be simplified. For instance, it is not essential to see the Grand High Witch's huge upside-down face under the bed. But it would be a shame not to include this highly theatrical moment.

CHARACTERS

Narrator

Boy: dressed as a mouse, but with his human face visible

Bruno Jenkins: similarly dressed as a mouse

Maid: wearing a black dress and white maid's cap. It would be possible not to see, only to hear her

Grandmother: wearing a dress and apron or (because she is convalescing) a dressing-gown

Two puppet mice: to represent Boy and Bruno. They

must be large enough to be seen on top of Grandmother's dressing-table, operated by the actors hidden
behind. They could be hand puppets or puppets on
short rods

The off-stage voice of the Grand High Witch, if
possible speaking into a microphone

Frog: an actor in a frog costume, to be a similar size to
Boy-Mouse. Instead of one Frog, it would be possible
to use several.

SETTING

An empty space for Boy-Mouse's journeys, behind
which is Grandmother's hotel bedroom and, alongside, the area underneath the Grand High Witch's
bed. Two curtains at the back of the stage area have a
gap between them to suggest the doorway to the bedroom. A platform or rostrum for the bedroom allows
the mouse puppets to be manipulated from behind the
dressing-table. A stool and a bed. The balcony can be
imagined at the front of the platform. A bed-leg could
be enough to suggest the Grand High Witch's bed,
only a section of which we need see. A huge painting
of the upside-down head of the Grand High Witch
could be behind the curtain, ready to be revealed
when she looks under the bed.

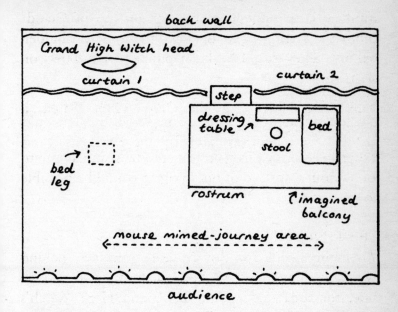

PROPS

Bruno's chunk of bread.

Grandmother's knitting: a large sock using three needles.

A fruit bowl, with bananas.

A potion-bottle, nearly as tall as a Boy-Mouse: this could be a cardboard cut-out.

SOUND EFFECTS

Optional music or percussion to accompany the mimed journeys of the Boy-Mice.

A door slam, footsteps, a cat's miaow: these would best be recorded.

The voice of the Grand High Witch would best be
live, spoken into a microphone.
Another door slam.

LIGHTING
No special lighting effects are required, but it would
be effective to light separately the three areas used and
cross-fade between them.

THE BOY-MOUSE

NARRATOR: Boy and his Grandmother are staying in Bournemouth at the Hotel Magnificent, which just happens to be the venue for the Witches of England's Annual Meeting, attended by the Grand High Witch of all the World. She has a plan to get rid of all the children of England. A delayed-action magic potion is to be injected into chocolate and sweets. When children eat them, they will turn into mice as soon as they get to school. Their teachers will use mousetraps to kill the mice, not realizing they are really children. Boy and greedy Bruno Jenkins have been used by the Grand High Witch to demonstrate her mouse-maker formula . . .

[*Curtain up*]

[*Enter* BOY, *dressed as a mouse. He scampers in and sniffs around, then looks about*]

BOY: [*Calling*] Bruno! Bruno Jenkins!

[*No reply.* BOY *frisks around happily*]

[*To the audience*] I should be sad. I should feel desperate. I mean, I've never dreamed of being a mouse, like I've dreamed of being, say, a film star. But now that I *am* one, I'm beginning to see the advantages. I know mice sometimes get poisoned or caught in traps but boys sometimes get killed too — run over or get some awful illness. Boys have to go to school. Mice don't. Mice don't have to pass exams. When mice grow up they don't have to go out to work. Mmm. It's no bad thing to be a mouse. I'm as free as William and Mary. Hope they're all right.

[BRUNO, *dressed as a mouse, enters eating a chunk of bread*]

Hello, Bruno.
[BRUNO *nods*]

What have you found?

BRUNO: An ancient fish–paste sandwich. Pretty good. Bit pongy.

BOY: Listen, Bruno. Now we're both mice, I think we ought to start thinking about the future.
[BRUNO *stops eating*]

BRUNO: What do you mean, we? The fact that you're a mouse has nothing to do with me.

BOY: But you're a mouse, too, Bruno.

BRUNO: Don't be stupid, I'm not a mouse.

BOY: I'm afraid you are, Bruno.

BRUNO: I most certainly am not. You're lying. I am most definitely not a mouse.

BOY: Look at your paws.

BRUNO: You're barmy! My paws? [*He looks at them*]

Aaaaah! They're all hairy. [*He feels his ears and whiskers*] Ugh! I *am* a mouse. [*He bursts into tears*]

BOY: The witches did it.

BRUNO: I don't want to be a mouse! [*He cries some more*]

BOY: Don't be silly, Bruno. There are worse things than being a mouse. You can live in a hole.

BRUNO: I don't want to live in a hole.

BOY: And you can creep into the larder at night and nibble through all the packets of biscuits and corn-flakes and stuff. You can stuff yourself silly.

BRUNO: [*Perking up*] Well, that's a thought. But how can I open the fridge door to get at the cold chicken and leftovers? I do that every evening at home.

BOY: Maybe your rich father will get you a special little mouse-fridge all to yourself. One you can open.

BRUNO: [*Sudden thought*] My father. What's he going to say? And my ma. She hates mice. [*Wailing*] What are we going to do?

BOY: We'll go and see my grandmother. She'll understand. She knows all about witches.

BRUNO: What's all this about witches? Which witches?

BOY: The witches who turned us into mice. The Grand High Witch gave you the chocolate, remember?

BRUNO: What, her? The miserable old bat.

BOY: Yes, well. Follow me to Grandmother's room. Down the corridor, run like mad.

BRUNO: B–b–but . . .

BOY: No talking. And don't let anyone see you. Don't forget that anyone who catches sight of you will try to kill you!

BRUNO: [*Terrified*] Ooooh!

BOY: Come on.

[*Optional music or percussion accompanies the mimed journey of* BOY *and* BRUNO *to* GRANDMOTHER's *room. First they scuttle along imaginary walls, occasionally stopping to check that the coast is clear. They edge cautiously round imaginary corners, then set off again along another wall.* BRUNO *lags behind and has to be encouraged and even pushed!*]

[*Suddenly a door-slam booms out, making them stop in alarm. Then footsteps echo as somebody walks along the corridor.* BOY *and* BRUNO *cover their eyes until the footsteps fade away. They set off again*]

[*Suddenly a loud cat miaow halts them in their tracks. They back away, then turn and escape round a corner. They exit*]

NARRATOR: At last Boy and Bruno found themselves in the corridor outside Grandmother's bedroom.
[*The scene changes to* GRANDMOTHER*'s hotel bedroom.* GRANDMOTHER *enters and sits on the bed, knitting a large sock with three needles*]
[*A female scream from outside her door makes her jump. She puts down her knitting, goes to the door and looks out*]

GRANDMOTHER: What on earth is going on out here?
[*A* MAID *pops her head round the door*]

MAID: Beg your pardon, madam. I thought I saw a mouse. Aaaaah!
[*She exits and her footsteps are heard as she runs away*]

BOY'S VOICE: [*Off*] Grandmamma! It's me, Boy! Down here.
[GRANDMOTHER *looks down at the floor outside the door and gasps*]

The witch got me.

GRANDMOTHER: The witch?
[GRANDMOTHER *picks up the puppet* BOY-MOUSE *and brings him into the room. She is shocked and starts to cry*]

BOY'S VOICE: Don't cry, Grandmamma. Things could be a lot worse. I'm still alive. So's Bruno. The witch got him too. He's in the corridor.

[GRANDMOTHER *bends down outside the door, to pick up* BRUNO-MOUSE. *She enters the room and puts both mice on the dressing-table. The actors, unseen behind, manipulate the puppets*]

[GRANDMOTHER *sits, stunned*]

[*Suddenly* BRUNO *sees a bowl of fruit*]

BRUNO'S VOICE: Mmm. Bananas. I like bananas. Can you peel one for me, please?

[GRANDMOTHER, *almost in a trance, gets up and peels one for him*]

Mmm! [*He makes eating noises*]

[*Pause as* GRANDMOTHER *sits again*]

BOY'S VOICE: Say something, Grandmamma.

GRANDMOTHER: Oh, my darling Boy, my poor sweet darling. What has she done to you?

BOY'S VOICE: It's all right, Grandmamma, really. I'm getting used to it. It's quite fun when you get the hang of it.

GRANDMOTHER: Where did it happen? Where is the witch now? Is she in the hotel?

BOY'S VOICE: Room four-five-four. She's the Grand High Witch of all the World.

GRANDMOTHER: The Grand High Witch, here?

BOY'S VOICE: Yes. And there are masses of other witches in the hotel too.

GRANDMOTHER: You don't mean they're having their Annual Meeting here?

BOY'S VOICE: They've had it, Grandmamma. I was there! Hiding. They call themselves the Royal Society for the Prevention of Cruelty to Children.

GRANDMOTHER: Huh! Typical! And how did they catch you, my darling?

BOY'S VOICE: They sniffed me out.

GRANDMOTHER: Mmm. Dogs' droppings, was it?

BOY'S VOICE: Yes. And then the Grand High Witch demonstrated her new magic formula. It turns children into mice.

GRANDMOTHER: I can see that, my darling, only too well.

BOY'S VOICE: But Grandmamma, they plan to turn all the children of England into mice.

GRANDMOTHER: The vicious creatures. That's English witches for you.

BOY'S VOICE: We've got to stop them!

GRANDMOTHER: Impossible. Witches are un-stoppable. They've got you. Now they'll get the others.

[Short pause]

BRUNO'S VOICE: Can you peel me another banana, please?

GRANDMOTHER: [*Peeling one*] Doesn't he ever stop eating?

BOY'S VOICE: No. [*Suddenly*] And that's another thing, Grandmamma, Bruno's parents. They don't know he's a mouse.

GRANDMOTHER: I can deal with that. But stopping the witches' grand plan is another kettle of fish.
[*Suddenly a voice is heard.* GRANDMOTHER *and* BOY *react as if it is coming from below them*]

GRAND HIGH WITCH'S VOICE:
Down with children! Do them in!
Boil their bones and fry their skin!
[*She cackles, then chants the rest, her voice getting softer, while* BOY *and* GRANDMOTHER *continue their conversation*]

Bish them, sqvish them, bash them, mash them!
Brrreak them, shake them, slash them, smash them!

BOY'S VOICE: It's her, Grandmamma, it's her!

GRANDMOTHER: The Grand High Witch?
[*She goes out on to her balcony and looks down, then returns*]

[*Furious*] Would you believe it? The evil woman is in the room below mine! I can see her balcony! The doors into her bedroom are open.

[*We hear a muffled cackle from the* GRAND HIGH WITCH]

BOY'S VOICE: [*Having an idea*] Grandmamma, if she's down there, so is her magic formula.

GRANDMOTHER: Well?

BOY'S VOICE: [*Working out his plan*] If I could only steal one tiny bottle. Five hundred doses! Works on grown-ups as well as children, she said. So who's to say it wouldn't work on *witches*? Don't you see?

GRANDMOTHER: [*Slowly*] I do! I do see.

BOY'S VOICE: Witches who are meeting for dinner at eight o'clock tonight!

GRANDMOTHER: Then there's no time to waste. My brilliant, darling, daring Boy.

BOY'S VOICE: Mouse.

GRANDMOTHER: Boy-Mouse, then. [*Declaiming*] For the salvation of the children of England. Action!
[*Optional exciting music as* GRANDMOTHER *swings into action. Meanwhile* BRUNO *continues attacking the fruit bowl. From now on* GRANDMOTHER *acts out the* NARRATOR'*s words*]

NARRATOR: Grandmother thought hard. Suddenly she had a brilliant idea. She took the sock she was knitting and carefully placed the Boy-Mouse inside it. Then, unravelling the ball of wool, she carefully lowered it to the balcony below.

GRANDMOTHER: [*Calling*] Out you get! Hurry up!
[*The* NARRATOR *enters the scene and removes the mouse puppet from the sock*]

NARRATOR: The Boy-Mouse climbed out of the sock and scuttled into the Grand High Witch's bedroom.
[*The* NARRATOR *exits, carrying the mouse puppet*]

GRAND HIGH WITCH'S VOICE: Vot is this knitting-vool hanging down here?

GRANDMOTHER: [*Innocently*] Oh, hello. I just dropped it over the balcony by mistake. So sorry. I've still got hold of one end, so I can pull it up.
[*She starts to pull up the wool*]

GRAND HIGH WITCH'S VOICE: Who vur you talking to just now? Who vur you telling to get out and hurry up?

GRANDMOTHER: [*Retrieving her knitting, now empty*] My little grandson. He's er . . . been in the bath for ages, reading his book, the little darling. It's time he got out. Do you have any children, my dear?

GRAND HIGH WITCH'S VOICE: Certainly not!
[*The sound of the balcony door slamming shut*]
[GRANDMOTHER *looks concerned*]

GRANDMOTHER: [*Fervently*] Good fortune be with you, my darling Boy-Mouse.

[*She sits on the bed as the scene changes to underneath the* GRAND HIGH WITCH'*s bed*]

NARRATOR: [*Entering*] The Boy-Mouse carefully explored the Grand High Witch's bedroom.
[BOY-MOUSE (*the actor in mouse-costume*) *enters, treading gingerly*]
[*He freezes when suddenly the* GRAND HIGH WITCH, *idly chanting, is heard booming overhead*]

GRAND HIGH WITCH'S VOICE:
Down with children! Do them in!
Boil their bones and fry their skin!
Bish them, sqvish them, bash them, mash them!
Brrreak them, shake them, slash them, smash them!
[*In the lull that follows, the* BOY-MOUSE *scuttles across, but jumps as he hears a manic cackle from the* GRAND HIGH WITCH. *He arrives under the bed*]

NARRATOR: The Boy-Mouse found himself under the Grand High Witch's bed!
[*The* GRAND HIGH WITCH *happily hums a version of her chant. It echoes in sinister fashion. Suddenly, out jumps a creature. It grabs* BOY-MOUSE, *but not roughly. Nevertheless,* BOY-MOUSE *jumps*]

BOY-MOUSE: Aaah!
[*The creature is a* FROG. *He springs away, trembling*]

Hello.
[*He advances. The* FROG *backs away*]

Hey, Frog. I won't hurt you.

[*He stretches out a paw. The* FROG *huddles up, enjoying the company*]

What are you doing here? Did the Grand High Witch magic you too?
[*The* FROG *nods*]

You were once a child?
[*The* FROG *nods*]

Have you never tried to escape?
[*The* FROG *shakes its head, fearful*]

You're frightened of her?
[*The* FROG *nods*]

So am I. Listen, Frog, do you know where she keeps her magic-formula bottles?
[*After a thinking pause the* FROG *points offstage, to further under the bed*]

Thanks, Frog.
[*He exits, briefly, returning with a potion bottle nearly his size. He starts to walk back the way he came but suddenly drops the bottle*]

Aaaaah!

GRAND HIGH WITCH'S VOICE: Vot vas that? I heard a noise.
[*Suddenly the curtain behind swings back to reveal the huge upside-down face of the* GRAND HIGH WITCH *peering under the bed*]

[BOY-MOUSE *manages to drag the bottle into a dark area. The* FROG *is there*]

Vas that you, little frrroggy? Making a noise? Are you being good? Guarding my magic bottles? Are you being a good votch-frrrog? [*She cackles*] Soon I vill be giving my bottles away and you need guard them no longer.

[*The* FROG *looks chirpier*]

Then I vill thrrrow you out of the vindow and the seagulls can have you for supper-time snacks! [*She cackles*]

[*The* FROG *trembles. A knock at the bedroom door is heard*]

Ah-a. The ancient vitches come for their potion bottles. [*She calls*] I come.

[*The curtain drops, covering her face*]

[BOY-MOUSE, *with the bottle, starts his journey again. He looks back at the trembling* FROG]

Come on, Frog!

[*They both escape downstage and, facing front, walk on the spot*]

NARRATOR: [*Entering*] The Boy-Mouse led the Frog safely to the back door of the hotel.

BOY-MOUSE: Off you go, Frog. You're free!

[FROG *hops off.* BOY-MOUSE *waves, then looks at the potion bottle*]

NARRATOR: Then he started planning to give the witches, and especially the Grand High Witch, a taste of their own medicine!

[*Curtain down*]

THE BOY-MOUSE
DEFEATS THE WITCHES

This play involves the transformation of the witches into mice! It requires as many as thirty actors, a reasonably large acting area, and a considerable number of props. Some of these will need to be specially made. The puppet mice can be soft toys. The trick soup-tureen and trolley are not essential but highly effective. The play uses slow-motion mime, which is highly theatrical and fun to do.

CHARACTERS

Narrator: who also operates the Boy-Mouse puppet

Head Waiter: wearing white bow-tie and coat with tails

Waiters, waitresses: one or two of each, wearing formal dress

Diners: a party of three or four, dressed smartly

Grandmother: wearing an evening dress and possibly a shawl

Boy and Bruno Jenkins: both are played by puppet mice, but we hear their human voices. The puppets could be glove puppets, but model, 'soft toy' mice would be suitable too

The Grand High Witch: smartly dressed for dinner, all in black; her horrid, wizened face (the actress's face made up) is covered by a pleasant-looking mask; she wears gloves and a bald wig covered by a black wig

The Witches: fifteen would be ideal, as long as they can all sit at the table; smartly dressed for dinner, wearing gloves and wigs (in this play their bald wigs are not required)

Head Chef and Second Chef: wearing white overalls and chef's hats; the Second Chef wears brightly coloured 'long johns' under his trousers

Mr Jenkins: dressed in a suit and flashy tie

Mrs Jenkins: dressed somewhat vulgarly with lots of over-the-top jewellery.

SETTING

This play needs a large space or stage. The hotel dining-room has two imagined doors offstage on one side: one is the main entrance, the other leads to the kitchen. On the other side is Grandmother's table and another table upstage. The Witches' long table is upstage centre. All the tables have cloths reaching to the floor. Downstage is enough room to accommodate the kitchen scene: this comprises a counter and dresser, both of which could be on castors. The counter has a hob and a work surface; the soup saucepan and other pots are on the hob; rolling pins and other utensils are on the work surface. The dresser has a work top and at least one shelf above, with pots and plates.

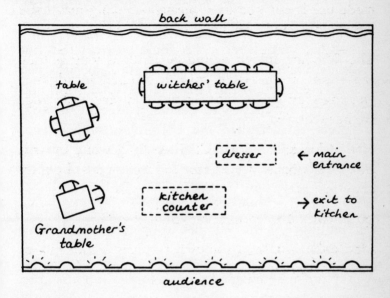

PROPS

Gong and beater (Head Waiter).

Plates, soup bowls and cutlery.

Small pad and pencil (Head Waiter).

Grandmother's handbag, which has to accommodate the two puppet mice; it could be a knitting bag or a carpet bag.

A small blue potion bottle, held by the Boy-Mouse puppet.

Baskets of bread rolls.

Menus, vases of flowers on the tables.

Pots and pans for the kitchen scene; rolling pins, ladles, meat slices, peas, carrots, gravy jug.

Large silver soup-tureen; this could be a cut-out, but ideally would be a custom-built prop, especially if it is to be entered by the Grand High Witch. It should stand on a trolley with castors; a hole in the top, slightly smaller than the bottomless soup-tureen, allows the Grand High Witch to descend into it; the trolley may need a false top to disguise the hole.

Enamel plates and pots for the dresser shelf.

Puppet mice for the Witches to operate from behind the tables.

A grey-green bedraggled puppet mouse (on a rod) to emerge from the soup-tureen.

SOUND EFFECTS

Background music in the dining-room should be unobtrusive. It could be recorded or live.

Eight loud clock chimes.

Kitchen sounds: the banging of pots and pans, food mixer whirring, etc.; could be live or recorded.

Possible music or percussion to accompany the chefs' slapstick scene.

A cacophony of distorted bells and chimes to accompany the transformation of the witches into mice; recorded or live.

For clarity, Boy and Bruno's voices should ideally be
amplified.

LIGHTING
It would be effective to be able to light three areas and
cross-fade between them:
• bright light for the whole dining-room;
• bright light for the kitchen only;
• dim lighting, an eerie green or blue, perhaps, on the
witches' table and downstage during the transformation scene.

One or two smoke machines would help cover the
witches' transformation.

THE BOY-MOUSE DEFEATS
THE WITCHES

NARRATOR: Boy and his Grandmother are staying in Bournemouth at the Hotel Magnificent. The Witches of England's Annual Meeting, attended by the Grand High Witch of all the World, is taking place there too. The Grand High Witch turns Boy and greedy Bruno Jenkins into mice, to demonstrate the powers of her latest magic potion. Soon the Witches will use the potion to get rid of all the children of England . . . unless the Boy-Mouse and his Grandmother can stop them. The Boy-Mouse has managed to steal a bottle of the potion. Grandmother takes him and Bruno, safely tucked in her handbag, to the hotel dining-room.

[*The* NARRATOR *exits as the* HEAD WAITER *enters, carrying a gong and beater*]

HEAD WAITER: [*After beating the gong a few times*] Ladies and gentlemen, dinner is served.

[*Curtain up*]

[*Background music plays as* WAITERS *and* WAITRESSES *finish laying tables and hover, waiting for the guests to arrive. The* HEAD WAITER *checks that all is ready, then exits to leave his dinner gong offstage*]

[*A party of* DINERS *enters. A* WAITER *approaches*]

WAITER: Good-evening, ladies. Good-evening, gentlemen.

DINERS: Good-evening.

WAITER: Please follow me. [*He leads them to their table and sits them down. A* WAITRESS *comes to take their order*]
  [GRANDMOTHER *enters. She holds, carefully, her large handbag in which are the two* BOY-MICE. *She waits until the* WAITER *approaches*]

Good-evening, madam.

GRANDMOTHER: Good-evening.

WAITER: Your table is this way.

GRANDMOTHER: Thank you.
  [*He leads her to her table, set with two chairs. She sits on one and carefully rests her handbag on the table*]
  [*The* WAITER *departs to help a* WAITRESS *lay plates on the* WITCHES' *table*]
  [*The* HEAD WAITER *enters and approaches* GRAND-MOTHER *with his notepad and pencil*]

HEAD WAITER: Good-evening, madam.

GRANDMOTHER: Good-evening.

HEAD WAITER: Where is the young gentleman tonight?

GRANDMOTHER: He's not feeling quite himself. He's staying in his room.

HEAD WAITER: I'm sorry to hear that. Now, this evening, to start with there is green pea soup, and for the main course you have a choice of either grilled fillet of sole or roast lamb.

GRANDMOTHER: Pea soup and lamb for me, please.

HEAD WAITER: Thank you, madam.

GRANDMOTHER: Thank you!
[*The* HEAD WAITER *leaves, heading for the kitchen*]
[GRANDMOTHER *surreptitiously speaks into her handbag*]

Ready, my darling? Have you got the bottle?

BOY'S VOICE: Yes. Grandmamma, what's the time?

GRANDMOTHER: [*Checking her watch*] It's five minutes to eight. We're just in time.
[*She carefully lowers the handbag to the floor, behind the table*]

Out you get. [*She takes out the* BOY-MOUSE *puppet and leaves it behind the table*] Stand by. Good luck!
[*She brings the handbag back up to the table*]

BRUNO'S VOICE: [*In the handbag*] I'm starving!

GRANDMOTHER: Quiet, Bruno. Have a bread roll.
[*She takes a roll from a basket and pops it in the handbag*]

BRUNO'S VOICE: It's got no butter!

GRANDMOTHER: [*Loudly*] Shut up!
[*The* WAITRESS *near by hears and looks round, startled, at* GRANDMOTHER, *who smiles sweetly*]
[*The* WAITRESS *starts to exit*]
[GRANDMOTHER *checks that the coast is clear, then looks down*]

Go, my darling, go!
[ALL *freeze as the* NARRATOR *enters*]

NARRATOR: [*Picking up* BOY-MOUSE, *who holds the potion bottle, and carrying him across to the other side*] The Boy-Mouse scuttled across the floor of the dining-room and found the door to the kitchen. As the Head Waiter came out, the Boy-Mouse slipped in.
[*The* NARRATOR *exits with* BOY-MOUSE, *as* ALL *unfreeze. The* WAITRESS *continues her journey to the kitchen, passing the* HEAD WAITER, *who carries the bowl of soup to* GRANDMOTHER'*s table*]

HEAD WAITER: Your green pea soup, madam.

GRANDMOTHER: Thank you. It smells most appetizing. [*She carefully places her handbag on the other chair*]
[*Suddenly the atmosphere changes. The music stops and eight loud clock chimes are heard. The* WITCHES *enter, led by the* GRAND HIGH WITCH *wearing her face-mask. They behave very charmingly*]

HEAD WAITER: [*Ultra polite*] Good-evening, ladies.

GRAND HIGH WITCH: Good-evening.

HEAD WAITER: Your table is this way.

[*The* HEAD WAITER *and the* WAITER *help them into their chairs.* GRANDMOTHER *watches. When all are settled the* HEAD WAITER *speaks*]

Tonight, ladies, there is green pea soup to start with, and for the main course you have a choice of either grilled fillet of sole or roast lamb.

[ALL *freeze as the lights fade down and loud kitchen sounds are heard: the banging of pots and pans, food mixer whirring, etc. This covers the change of scene to the kitchen. The* HEAD CHEF *and* SECOND CHEF *push their counter/hob and dresser/work top onstage. Meanwhile the* HEAD WAITER *exits*]

[*The lights fade up as the two* CHEFS *burst into activity. The* HEAD CHEF *stirs the soup and the* SECOND CHEF *bangs a slice of meat with a rolling-pin. Suddenly they freeze, as the* NARRATOR *enters, carrying* BOY-MOUSE]

NARRATOR: Meanwhile, in the kitchen, Boy-Mouse looked for a place to hide. Carefully carrying the magic-potion bottle, he climbed up to the shelf of the kitchen dresser. [*The* NARRATOR *manipulates* BOY-MOUSE *up the dresser and holds him on the shelf, peeping out from behind a plate. The* NARRATOR *stays behind the dresser, working the puppet*]

[*The* CHEFS *unfreeze and start stirring and banging again*]

[*A* WAITER *hurries in*]

WAITER: [*Shouting*] Two lamb for table four!

HEAD CHEF: Two lamb for table four!

SECOND CHEF: Two lamb for table four!
[*Working as a double act, they slap two plates on the counter*]

SECOND CHEF
HEAD CHEF } [*Together*] Meat!
  [*They slap a slice on each plate*]

SECOND CHEF
HEAD CHEF } [*Together, proudly*] Meat!

SECOND CHEF: Peas!

HEAD CHEF: Peas!
[*They plop a handful of peas on each plate*]

SECOND CHEF
HEAD CHEF } [*Together, proudly*] Peas!

HEAD CHEF: Carrots!

SECOND CHEF: Carrots!
[*They chuck a handful of carrots on each plate*]

SECOND CHEF
HEAD CHEF } [*Together, proudly*] Carrots!

SECOND CHEF: Gravy!

HEAD CHEF: Gravy!

[*He tips a gravy jug. It is empty*]

No gravy!

SECOND CHEF: No gravy!

HEAD CHEF: [*Idea*] Do-it-yourself gravy!

SECOND CHEF: Do-it-yourself gravy!
[*Each takes a plate and spits on it. Then they plump up the food with their fingers*]

SECOND CHEF ⎫ [*Together, proudly*] Two lamb for
HEAD CHEF ⎭ table four! [*Together to the* WAITER, *shouting*] Two lamb for table four!

WAITER: [*Taking the plates*] Two lamb for table four!
[*He exits, nearly bumping into the* HEAD WAITER *as he enters*]

HEAD WAITER: [*Shouting*] Everyone in the big RSPCC party wants the soup! [*He exits*]

HEAD CHEF: Soup for the big party!

SECOND CHEF: Soup for the big party!

HEAD CHEF: In the silver soup-tureen!

SECOND CHEF: In the silver soup-tureen!
[*They find it under the counter and place it on the dresser work top right under where* BOY-MOUSE *is hiding*]
[*As they return to their counter, suddenly they freeze.*

The NARRATOR *manipulates* BOY-MOUSE *to echo the narration*]

NARRATOR: Boy-Mouse saw his chance. He poured the potion into the soup-tureen. [*A magical tinkly sound. Having poured the potion, the* NARRATOR *makes* BOY-MOUSE *hide again*]
[*The* CHEFS *unfreeze*]

HEAD CHEF: Pour in the soup!

SECOND CHEF: Pour in the soup!
[*They take the saucepan and pour soup into the tureen. The soup can be imaginary if the pouring is masked by the saucepan*]

HEAD CHEF ⎱ [*Together*] Soup for the big party!
SECOND CHEF ⎰ [*They shout*] Soup for the big party!
[*The* HEAD WAITER *enters with a trolley. The* HEAD CHEF *and the* SECOND CHEF *place the soup-tureen on the trolley*]

HEAD WAITER: [*As he goes*] Soup for the big party!
[*The* HEAD WAITER *exits, pushing the trolley*]
[*Suddenly the* NARRATOR *makes* BOY-MOUSE *knock an enamel plate, which falls off the dresser, hitting the* SECOND CHEF *and revealing* BOY-MOUSE *on the shelf*]

SECOND CHEF: What was that?
[*He looks round and up*]

Hey, look! A mouse! A mouse!

HEAD CHEF: Where, where?

SECOND CHEF: There, there!
[*The* CHEFS *grab a rolling-pin and ladle and try to wallop* BOY-MOUSE, *who quickly hides behind a pot*]

He's hiding! He's hiding!

HEAD CHEF: There he goes!
[*They follow the imaginary progress of the mouse down the sides of the dresser, across to behind the counter. Slapstick fun as the* CHEFS *try to whack the mouse but only succeed in whacking each other and bumping into each other*]

Take that!

SECOND CHEF: Ow! Take that!

HEAD CHEF: Ow!
[*Suddenly the* SECOND CHEF *freezes in horror*]

SECOND CHEF: Eeeeee!

HEAD CHEF: What is it?

SECOND CHEF: Jeepers creepers! It's gone up my trouser leg! Ah! Ah! Oo! Oo!
[*He comes out from behind the counter, jumping up and down, slapping his trouser leg*]

Holy smoke! It's going all the way up! Ah! Oo! Help!
[*Now he is jumping up and down as though he is standing on hot bricks*]

Help! Help!
[*He stops suddenly*]

It's in my knickers! There's a mouse running around in my flaming knickers! Aaaah!

HEAD CHEF: Quick! Get 'em off!
[*He attacks the* SECOND CHEF, *trying to get his trousers off. The* SECOND CHEF *resists*]

SECOND CHEF: Stop it! Stop it! You're tickling! [*He giggles hysterically*]

HEAD CHEF: Off! Off!
[*Suddenly the* SECOND CHEF's *trousers drop, revealing funny underwear*]
[*The lights fade down as the kitchen scene clears, then come up on the dining-room as we left it with* GRANDMOTHER *at her table and the* WITCHES *awaiting their soup. The background music returns*]
[*The* WAITRESS *enters with rolls for the other diners*]

BRUNO'S VOICE: Can I have another roll, please?

GRANDMOTHER: [*Loudly towards her handbag*] Quiet, Bruno!
[*The* WAITRESS *hears and looks, startled, at* GRANDMOTHER, *who smiles sweetly. The* WAITRESS *exits*]
[GRANDMOTHER *picks up her handbag and drops another roll inside*]
[*The* HEAD WAITER *approaches* GRANDMOTHER, *sees her apparently stealing the roll, but discreetly ignores it*]

HEAD WAITER: Have you finished your green pea soup, madam?

GRANDMOTHER: Thank you, it was delicious.

HEAD WAITER: Thank *you*, madam. I'm glad you enjoyed it.
[*He starts to exit towards the kitchen, then freezes*]
[*The* NARRATOR *enters, carrying* BOY-MOUSE, *who no longer carries the potion bottle, and crossing to* GRANDMOTHER'*s table*]

NARRATOR: Boy-Mouse escaped from the kitchen and hurried back along the dining-room floor.
[*The* NARRATOR *kneels down and places* BOY-MOUSE *behind the table. The* HEAD WAITER *unfreezes and exits*]

BOY'S VOICE: Grandmamma, I'm back! Mission accomplished!
[GRANDMOTHER *picks him up and puts him on the table, hidden from general view by a menu or a vase of flowers. The* NARRATOR *continues to manipulate him*]

GRANDMOTHER: Well *done*, my darling. Well done, you.

BOY'S VOICE: Have the Witches arrived, Grandmamma?

GRANDMOTHER: They're over there, my darling. Look!
[*The* WITCHES *are talking animatedly*]

[*The* HEAD WAITER, *a* WAITER *and a* WAITRESS *enter, pushing the soup-tureen on its trolley*]

HEAD WAITER: Ladies, your green pea soup.
[*They arrive at the* WITCHES' *table and start to serve it as the focus returns to* GRANDMOTHER'*s table*]

BOY'S VOICE: They're going to drink it, Grand-mamma, they're going to drink it!
[BOY-MOUSE *bobs up and down*]

GRANDMOTHER: Shhh! Keep still. And cross your fingers.

BOY'S VOICE: I haven't got any fingers to cross.

GRANDMOTHER: Sorry. [*She smiles*]
[MR *and* MRS JENKINS *enter, scanning the restaurant. They see* GRANDMOTHER *and head towards her*]

BOY'S VOICE: Look out, Grandmamma. It's Bruno's parents.
[GRANDMOTHER *makes sure the puppet* BOY-MOUSE *is hidden from* MR *and* MRS JENKINS. *Meanwhile the* WITCHES *start drinking their soup. The* HEAD WAITER, WAITER *and* WAITRESS *hover*]

MR JENKINS: Where's that grandson of yours?

MRS JENKINS: We reckon he's up to something with our . . .

MR JENKINS
MRS JENKINS } [*Together*] Bruno.

MRS JENKINS: Some devilment.

MR JENKINS: The little beggar's not turned up for his supper. Most unlike him.

MRS JENKINS: Most unlike him.

GRANDMOTHER: I agree. He has a very healthy appetite.

MRS JENKINS: How do you know? Have you seen him? Where is he?

GRANDMOTHER: I'm afraid I have some rather alarming news for you. He's in my handbag.
   [*She holds it out.* MR *and* MRS JENKINS *can't believe their ears*]

MR JENKINS: What the heck d'you mean, he's in your handbag?

MRS JENKINS: Are you trying to be funny?

GRANDMOTHER: There's nothing funny about it. Your son has been rather drastically altered.

MR JENKINS
MRS JENKINS } [*Together*] Altered?

MR JENKINS: What the devil do you mean?

GRANDMOTHER: My own grandson actually saw them doing it to him.

MR JENKINS: Saw *who* doing *what* to him, for heaven's sake?

GRANDMOTHER: Saw the Witches turning him into a mouse.
[*The* JENKINSES' *mouths gape*]

MRS JENKINS: Call the manager, dear. Have this mad woman thrown out of the hotel.

GRANDMOTHER: [*Calmly*] Bruno is a mouse.

MR JENKINS: He most certainly is not a mouse!
[*Suddenly* GRANDMOTHER *delves into the handbag and pops* BRUNO-MOUSE's *head out. She moves him as he talks*]

BRUNO'S VOICE: Oh yes I am! Hello, Pa, Hello, Ma!
[MRS JENKINS *nearly screams. She and* MR JENKINS *back off nervously, horrified*]

MR JENKINS: B-b-b-b . . .

BRUNO'S VOICE: Don't worry, Pa. It's not as bad as all that. Just so long as the cat doesn't get me.

MR JENKINS: But I can't have a mouse for a son!

GRANDMOTHER: You've got one. Be nice to him.

MRS JENKINS: [*Approaching with difficulty*] My poor baby! Who did this?
[MRS JENKINS *picks up* BRUNO *in the handbag, trying to hide her distaste*]

GRANDMOTHER: That woman over there.
[*She points to the* GRAND HIGH WITCH]

Black dress. Finishing her soup.

MR JENKINS: She's RSPCC. The chairwoman.

GRANDMOTHER: No. She's the Grand High Witch of all the World.

MRS JENKINS: You mean *she* did it? That skinny woman over there?

MR JENKINS: What a nerve. I'll make her pay through the nose. I'll have my lawyers on to her for this.
 [*He turns towards the* GRAND HIGH WITCH]

GRANDMOTHER: I wouldn't do anything rash. That woman has magic powers. She might turn *you* into something. A cockroach, perhaps.

MR JENKINS: Turn *me* into a cockroach? I'd like to see her try!
 [*He sets off again. But he is stopped in his tracks by a very loud alarm bell. The lighting focuses on the* WITCHES' *table. It should create an eerie atmosphere. It is suggested that all the following action is performed* **in slow motion** *against a background of distorted clock and bell sounds*]
 [*The* GRAND HIGH WITCH *leaps in the air, on to her chair, then on to the table. She clutches her throat, aware that she has been poisoned. Smoke begins to swirl around the* WITCHES' *table.* WITCH 1 *and the other* WITCHES *start to leap up on the table too, others simply stand. All writhe about, waving their arms. The*

other DINERS, *the* HEAD WAITER, WAITRESSES
and WAITERS *as well as* GRANDMOTHER *and* MR
and MRS JENKINS *watch the* WITCHES' *behaviour
in awed amazement. The* GRAND HIGH WITCH
*climbs down from the table. She realizes the soup is
responsible for her behaviour and approaches the tureen
in fury. The* HEAD WAITER, *terrified, pushes the
tureen trolley towards her in self-defence. The* GRAND
HIGH WITCH *avoids the trolley, which collides into*
MR JENKINS. *As the other* WITCHES *start to
'shrink', still writhing helplessly, the* GRAND HIGH
WITCH *advances downstage. She removes her wig and
face-mask, revealing her horrid face to the audience,
then turns upstage. The other* DINERS, *the* HEAD
WAITER, WAITRESSES, WAITERS, GRAND-
MOTHER *and* MR *and* MRS JENKINS *react in horror.
The* HEAD WAITER *and* MR JENKINS *advance
towards the* GRAND HIGH WITCH, *who evades
them, but finds her only escape route is over the trolley.
She climbs up on it. The* HEAD WAITER *and* MR
JENKINS *try to reach her, forcing her to step into the
tureen*]

[*Everyone watches as, screaming in a nightmarish echo,
the* GRAND HIGH WITCH *descends into the tureen
and disappears, a separate hand being the last part of
her to go. If a tureen trolley is not possible, the* GRAND
HIGH WITCH *could disappear with the other*
WITCHES, *but to give her a more horrible end than the
others is satisfying to the audience*]

[*Amazed, the others look on as the* HEAD WAITER

picks up the wig and face-mask that the GRAND HIGH WITCH *has dropped, and shows them around.* MR JENKINS *looks into the tureen and a mouse, covered in green pea soup, slowly appears from the tureen, looking at him and quivering with rage*]

[As MR JENKINS *and the* HEAD WAITER *clear the trolley away, we become aware that all the other* WITCHES *have vanished. They have hidden behind and under the tables or exited under cover of the smoke*]

[*Then puppet mice appear from behind the table and, if possible, in other places. The* WITCHES *have all been turned into mice.* MRS JENKINS *shows* BRUNO-MOUSE *the successful conclusion of* BOY-MOUSE's *plan*]

[*The action freezes as the* NARRATOR, *carrying* BOY-MOUSE, *steps forward and stands centre*]

NARRATOR: [*Holding up* BOY-MOUSE *in triumph*] The Boy-Mouse had saved the children of England.

[*Curtain down*]

SO LONG AS SOMEBODY LOVES YOU

This extremely short play is an intimate duologue between a human being and a puppet. It brings the story of *The Witches* to a moving conclusion.

CHARACTERS
Narrator

Grandmother: wearing her dress and apron

Boy: he is not seen, but heard; hidden behind the table, he operates the Boy-Mouse puppet. A glove puppet or a rod puppet is possible, or a soft toy.

SETTING
Grandmother's table and chair.

PROPS
Grandmother's embroidery.

SOUND EFFECTS
For clarity, Boy's voice should be amplified.
The gentle ticking of a clock could add atmosphere.

LIGHTING
No special lighting effects are required.

SO LONG AS SOMEBODY LOVES YOU

NARRATOR: Boy and his Grandmother have defeated the Witches of England and the Grand High Witch of all the World. They have foiled their evil plan to turn all the children of England into mice. Instead, Boy and Grandmother have given the Witches a taste of their own medicine by turning *them* into mice! But their triumph is not total. In the course of the campaign, the Grand High Witch has turned Boy into a mouse. Grandmother takes him home to Norway where she can best look after him . . .

[*Curtain up*]

[GRANDMOTHER *sits in her chair, doing some embroidery. On her table alongside sits* BOY-MOUSE, *operated by* BOY, *hidden behind*]

BOY'S VOICE: Grandmamma, has the Grand High Witch really gone for ever?

GRANDMOTHER: Yes, my darling. But Grand High Witches are like queen bees. There's always another one to take over. Let's hope there are always people like you brave enough to foil their wicked plans.

BOY'S VOICE: Even if they end up as mice?

GRANDMOTHER: Even if they end up as mice.

[*Pause*]

BOY'S VOICE: Can I ask you something, Grandmamma?

GRANDMOTHER: Anything.

BOY'S VOICE: How long does a mouse live?

GRANDMOTHER: Not very long, I'm afraid. Just a few years.
[*Pause*]

BOY'S VOICE: And how much longer will you live, Grandmamma?

GRANDMOTHER: Just a few years.

BOY'S VOICE: Good. I'll be a very old mouse and you'll be a very old grandmother and we'll both die together.

GRANDMOTHER: That would be perfect.
[*Pause*]

My darling, are you sure you don't mind being a mouse for the rest of your life?

BOY'S VOICE: I don't mind at all. It doesn't matter who you are or what you look like, so long as somebody loves you.
[GRANDMOTHER'*s hand and the puppet* BOY-MOUSE'*s paw meet. They remain silent and happy together as the lights fade*]

[*Curtain down*]

Read more in Puffin

For complete information about books available from Puffin – and Penguin – and how to order them, contact us at the appropriate address below. Please note that for copyright reasons the selection of books varies from country to country.

www.puffin.co.uk

In the United Kingdom: Please write to Dept EP, Penguin Books Ltd,
Bath Road, Harmondsworth, West Drayton, Middlesex UB7 ODA

In the United States: Please write to Penguin Putnam Inc., P.O. Box 12289,
Dept B, Newark, New Jersey 07101–5289 or call 1–800–788–6262

In Canada: Please write to Penguin Books Canada Ltd,
10 Alcorn Avenue, Suite 300, Toronto, Ontario M4V 3B2

In Australia: Please write to Penguin Books Australia Ltd,
P.O. Box 257, Ringwood, Victoria 3134

In New Zealand: Please write to Penguin Books (NZ) Ltd,
Private Bag 102902, North Shore Mail Centre, Auckland 10

In India: Please write to Penguin Books India Pvt Ltd,
11 Panscheel Shopping Centre, Panscheel Park, New Delhi 110 017

In the Netherlands: Please write to Penguin Books Netherlands bv,
Postbus 3507, NL–1001 AH Amsterdam

In Germany: Please write to Penguin Books Deutschland GmbH,
Metzlerstrasse 26, 60594 Frankfurt am Main

In Spain: Please write to Penguin Books S. A., Bravo Murillo 19,
1° B, 28015 Madrid

In Italy: Please write to Penguin Italia s.r.l.,
Via Felice Casati 20, I–20124 Milano

In France: Please write to Penguin France S. A.,
17 rue Lejeune, F–31000 Toulouse

In Japan: Please write to Penguin Books Japan, Ishikiribashi Building,
2–5–4, Suido, Bunkyo-ku, Tokyo 112

In South Africa: Please write to Longman Penguin Southern Africa (Pty) Ltd,
Private Bag X08, Bertsham 2013